This book is intended for use in conjunction with beginner instrumental music lessons for treble clef instruments.

It is designed to assist students in learning to read music by providing activities that can be completed at home to reinforce what is learned during lessons. Activities are simple enough to be able to be completed by the youngest beginners.

Activities are numbered 1 through to 68, and do not need to be completed in the order set out in the book. Teachers may vary the order of the activities to support their own curriculum.

Contents

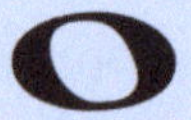

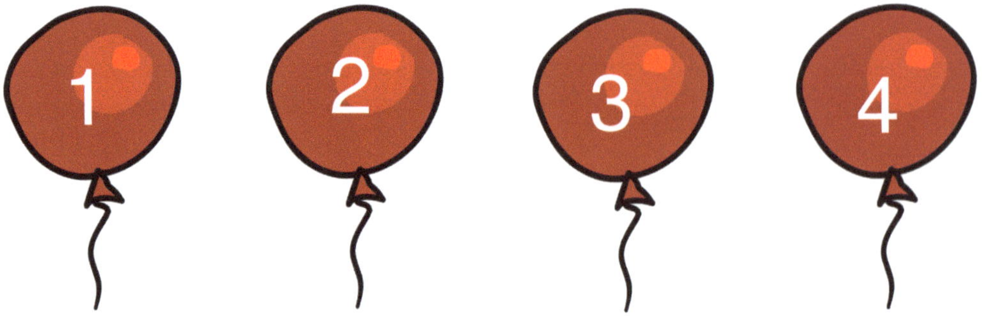

Note Name

SEMIBREVE or WHOLE NOTE

Rhythm Name

"Great Big Whole Note"

Sounds for

4 counts

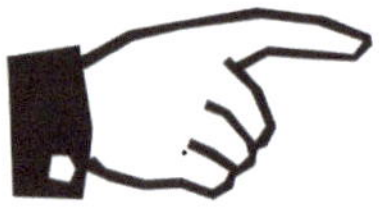

1. Notice how a semibreve (whole note) looks like a circle.

   Trace around the examples, then draw four more on the line:

2. Write the counts underneath (the first one is completed for you to copy):

   1 2 3 4

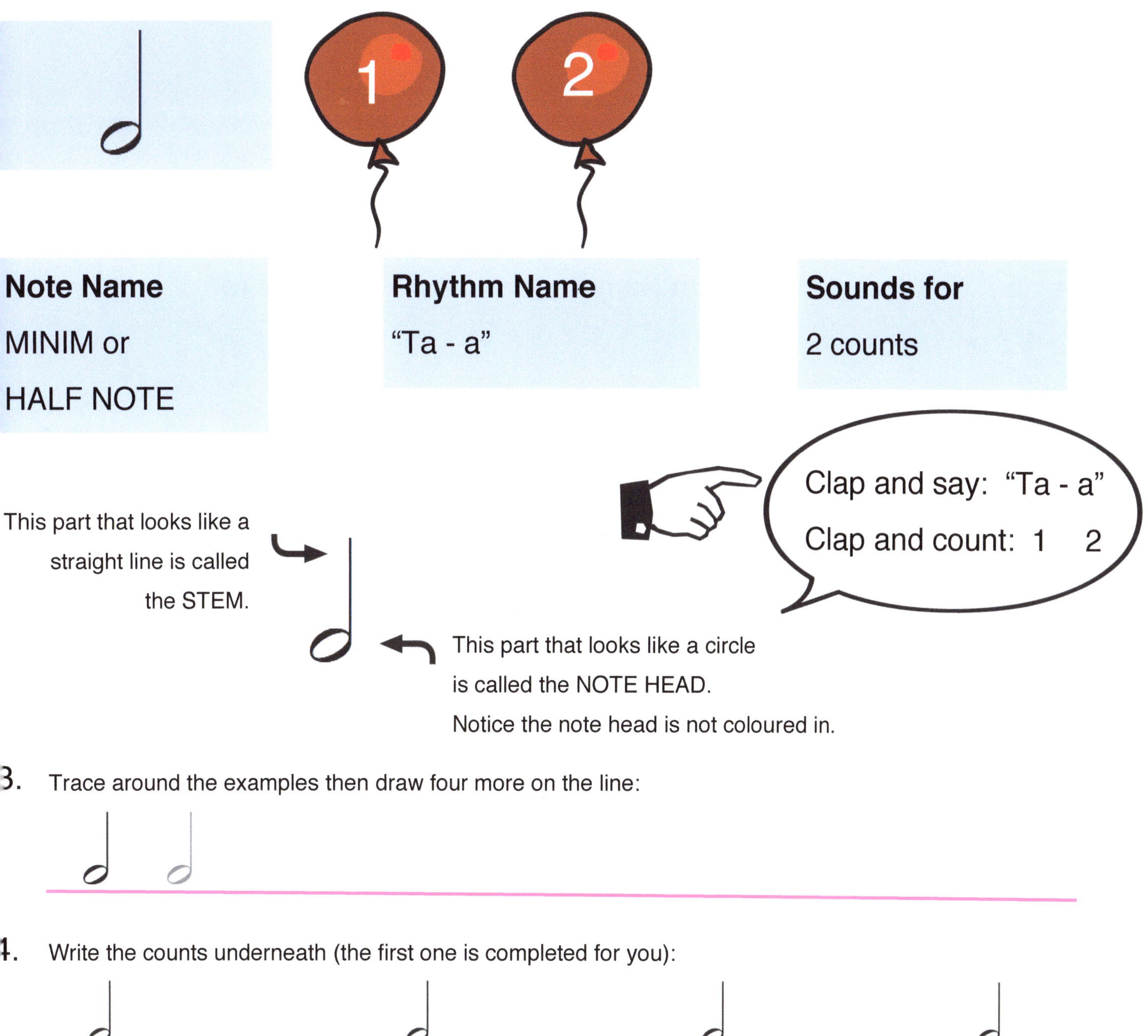

Note Name

MINIM or

HALF NOTE

Rhythm Name

"Ta - a"

Sounds for

2 counts

3.   Trace around the examples then draw four more on the line:

4.   Write the counts underneath (the first one is completed for you):

1   2

Note Values

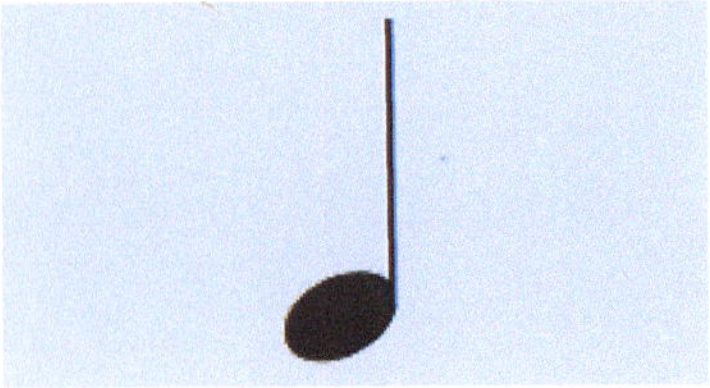

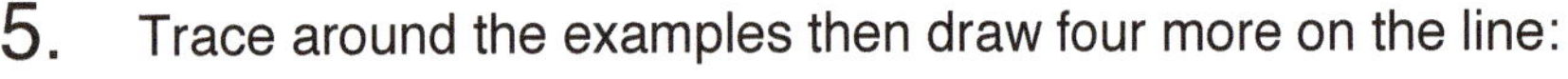

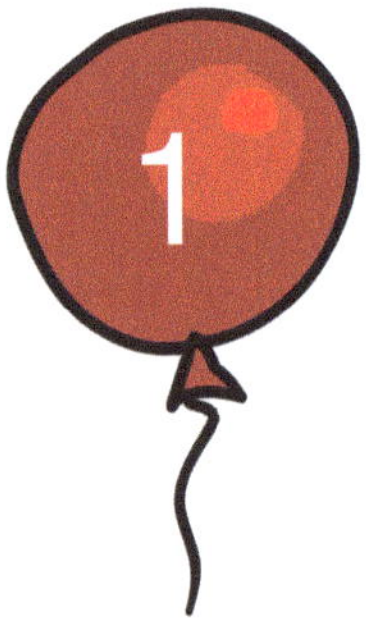
1

Note Name	Rhythm Name	Sounds for
CROTCHET or QUARTER NOTE	"Ta"	1 count

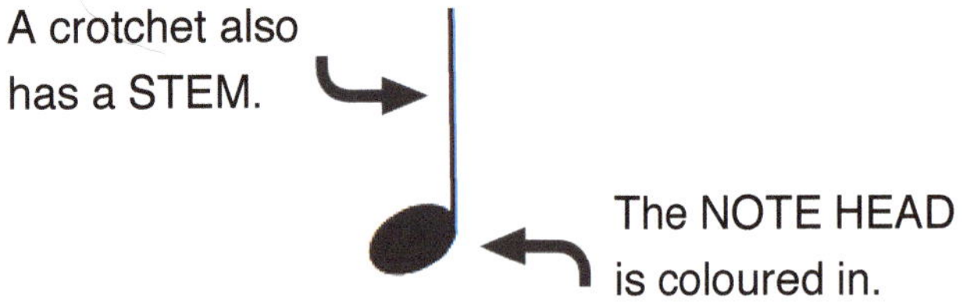
A crotchet also has a STEM.
The NOTE HEAD is coloured in.

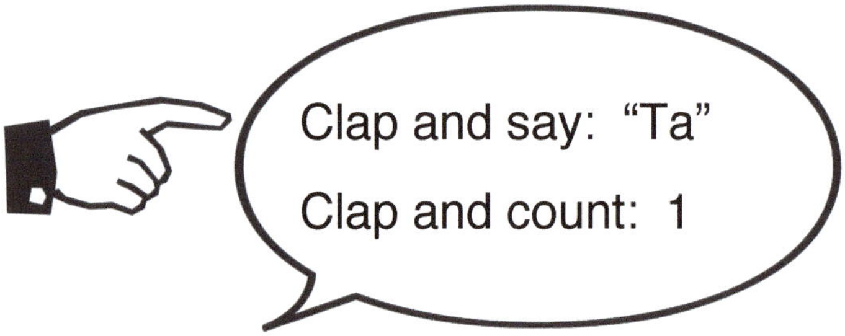
Clap and say: "Ta"
Clap and count: 1

5. Trace around the examples then draw four more on the line:

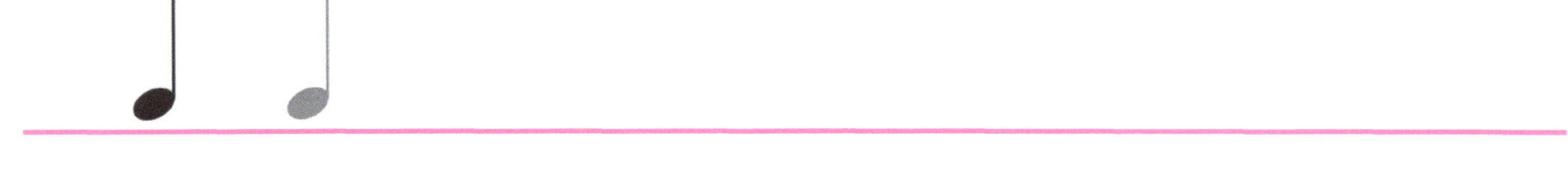

6. Write the counts underneath (the first one is completed for you to copy):

1

Note Values

Note Name	Rhythm Name	Sounds for
DOTTED MINIM or DOTTED HALF NOTE	"Ta - a - a"	3 counts

A dotted minim looks like a minim with a dot after it.

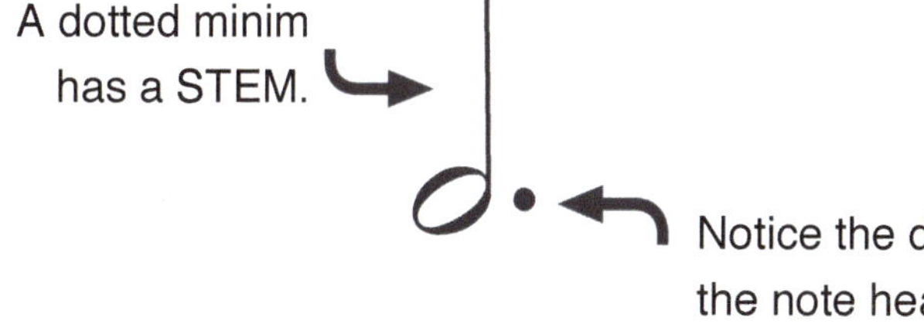

9. Draw four dotted minims on the line:

10. Write the counts under the dotted minims:

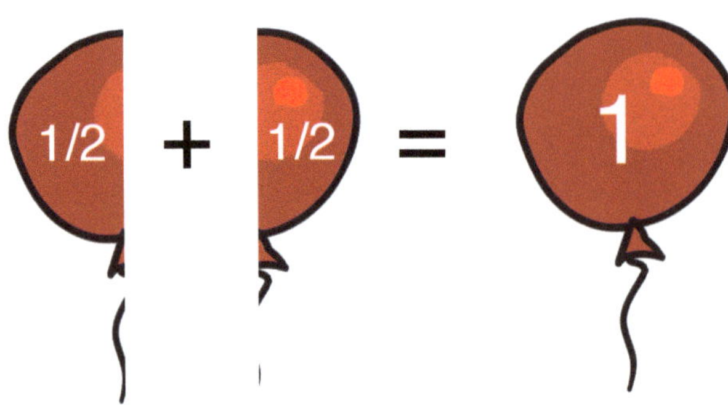

Note Name

QUAVERS or
EIGHTH NOTES

Rhythm Name

"Ti - ti"

Sounds for

Half a count each.

Two together take up one count.

The stems can go up or down.

24. Trace around the examples, then draw four pairs of quavers on the line:

25. Write the counts underneath (the first one is completed for you to copy):

1 and

Stems can go UP or DOWN.

UP stems go on the RIGHT of the note head.

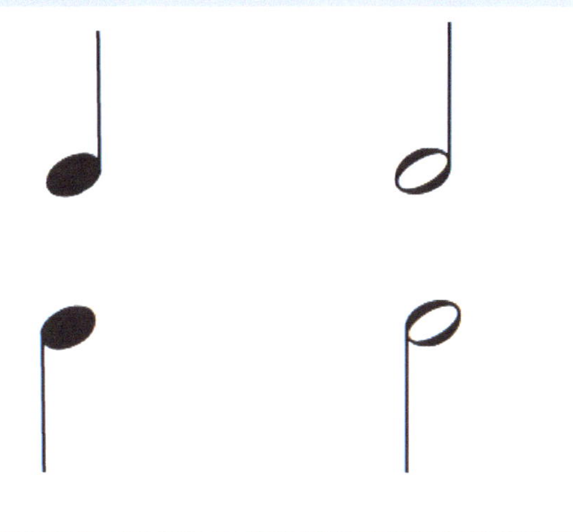

DOWN stems go on the LEFT of the note head.

7. Draw DOWN stems on the LEFT of these note heads.

8. Draw UP stems on the RIGHT of these note heads.

Musical Alphabet

In music, sounds (or pitches) are given a letter name.

The musical alphabet uses these letter names:

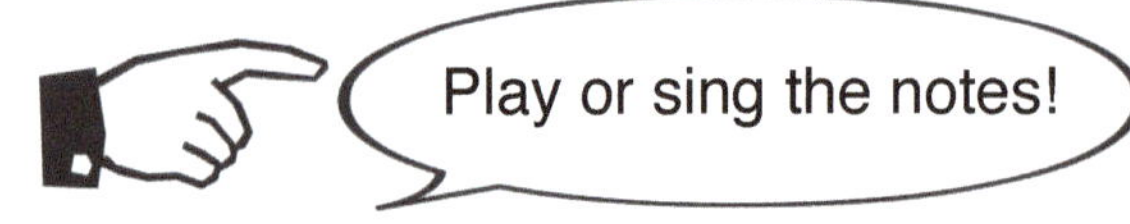

A B C D E F G

11. Fill in the missing letter names:

A □ C □ E F □

A □ □ D E □ G

□ B □ □ □ F □

A □ C □ □ □ G

Imagine the musical alphabet like a ladder.

You step up from one letter name to the next letter name.

When you get to G, the letter names start again from A.

As we climb UP the ladder the pitch of the notes gets HIGHER.

As we climb DOWN the ladder, the pitch of the notes gets LOWER.

12. Stepping DOWN. Fill in the blanks:

B steps DOWN to <u>A</u>

C steps DOWN to

G steps DOWN to __

D steps DOWN to __

F steps DOWN to __

Step up or down? Circle the correct answer.

13.

B to A is a step UP / DOWN   D to E is a step UP / DOWN

F to G is a step UP / DOWN   C to B is a step UP / DOWN

G to A is a step UP / DOWN   B to C is a step UP / DOWN

Musical Alphabet

The musical alphabet is like stairs, or a ladder. As we go up the stairs (or the ladder) the pitch of notes sounds HIGHER. As we go down the stairs, the notes sound LOWER.

When we go from one letter name to its next door neighbour, this is called a STEP.

You can step UP or DOWN.

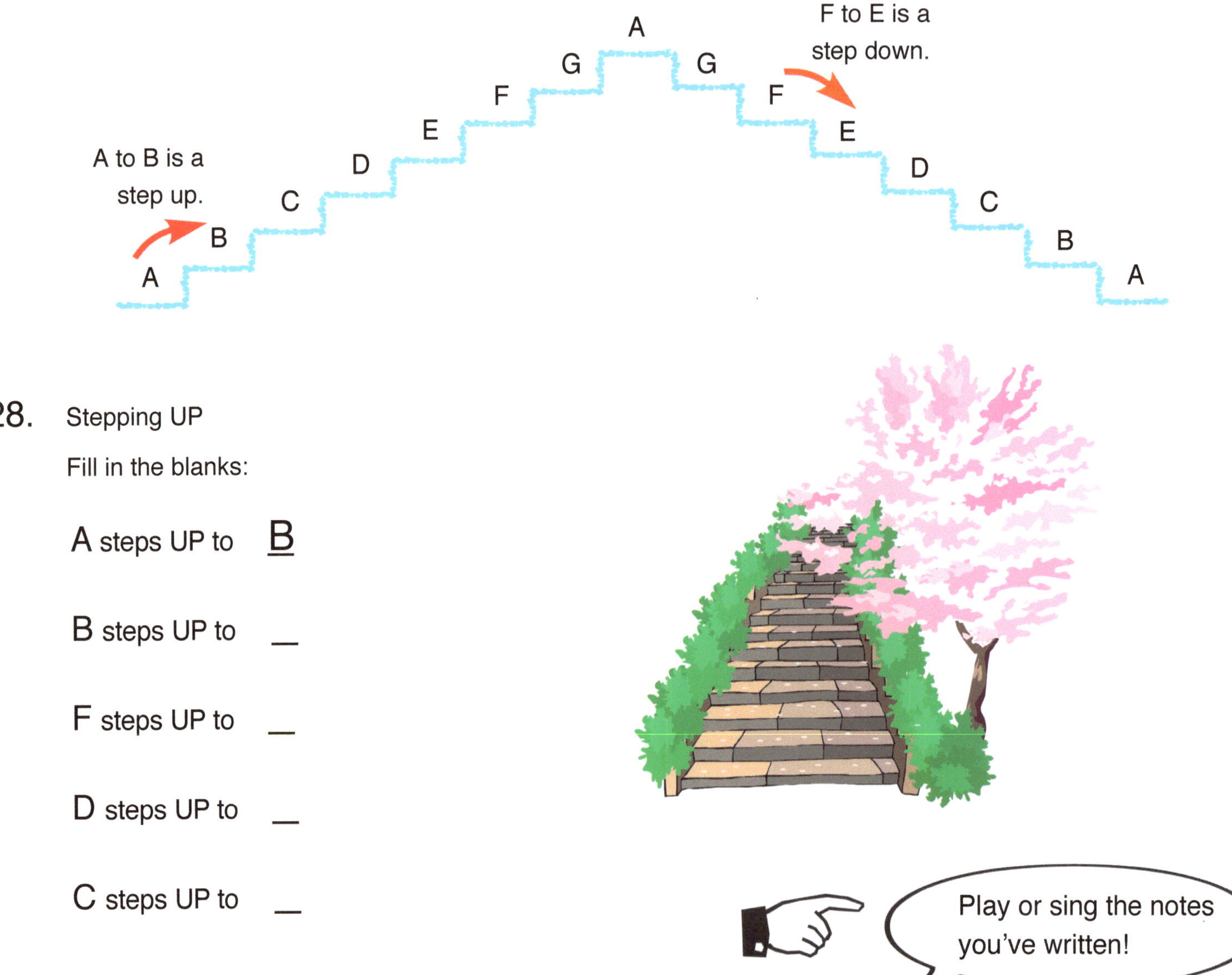

28.   Stepping UP

Fill in the blanks:

A steps UP to   <u>B</u>

B steps UP to   __

F steps UP to   __

D steps UP to   __

C steps UP to   __

Remember the musical alphabet is like stairs, or a ladder. As we go up the stairs the pitch sounds HIGHER. As we go down the stairs the pitch sounds LOWER.

When we go from one letter name to its next door neighbour, this is called a STEP.

When we skip over a letter name, this is called a SKIP (or a JUMP).

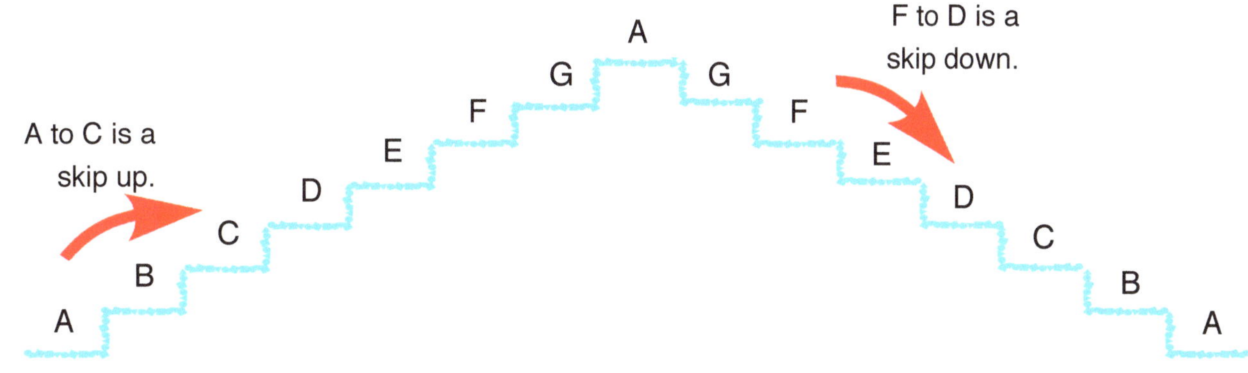

47. Skipping UP

Fill in the blanks:

A skips UP to C   A skips DOWN to F

B skips UP to _   B skips DOWN to _

F skips UP to _   G skips DOWN to _

D skips UP to _   C skips DOWN to _

C skips UP to _   D skips DOWN to _

48. Skipping UP and DOWN

Fill in the blanks:

B skips DOWN to <u>G</u>		B skips UP to <u>D</u>
C skips UP to ___		C skips DOWN to ___
G skips DOWN to ___		F skips UP to ___
D skips UP to ___		E skips DOWN to ___
F skips DOWN to ___		A skips UP to ___

49. Skips up or down? Circle the correct answer.

B to G is a skip UP / DOWN	D to B is a skip UP / DOWN
F to A is a skip UP / DOWN	C to E is a skip UP / DOWN
G to B is a skip UP / DOWN	B to D is a skip UP / DOWN

50. Circle the correct answer.

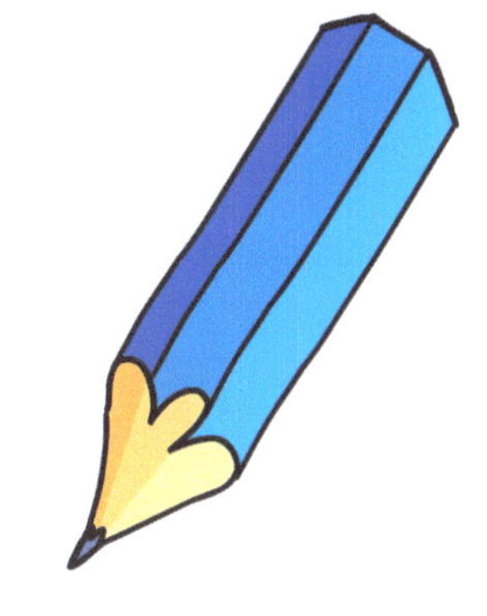

B to A is a   SKIP UP / STEP DOWN

A to F is a   SKIP DOWN / STEP DOWN

G to B is a   SKIP UP / STEP UP

A to C is a   SKIP UP / STEP DOWN

A to B is a   STEP DOWN / STEP UP

D to C is a   SKIP UP / STEP DOWN

C to E is a   STEP UP / SKIP UP

E to G is a   SKIP UP / SKIP DOWN

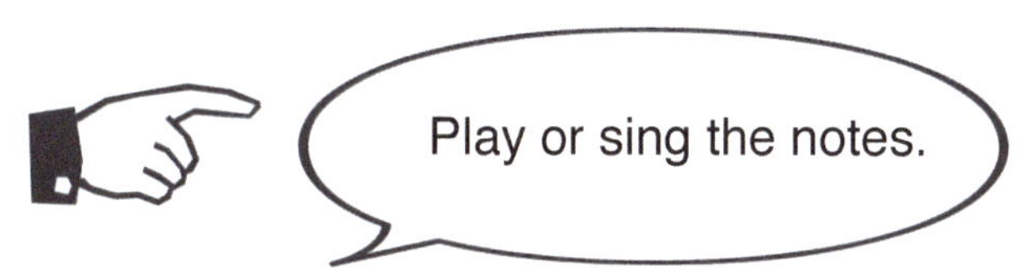

Time Signatures

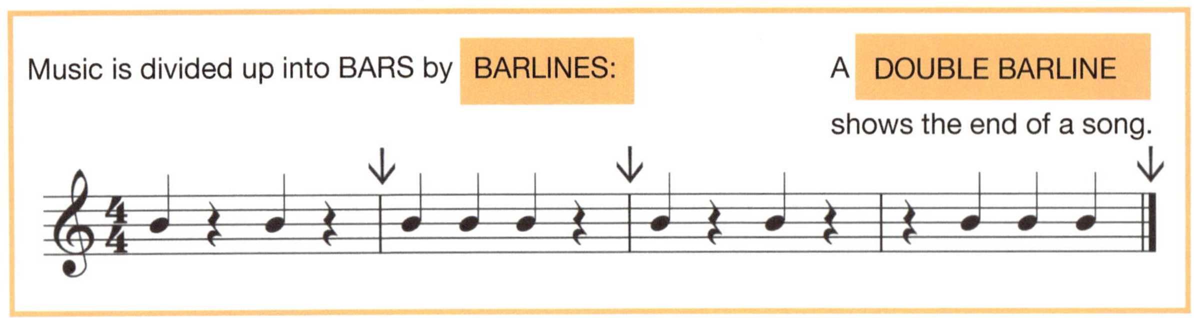

The numbers at the start of music are called the TIME SIGNATURE

The top number tells you how many beats are in each bar.

This time signature has a 4 on the top, so there are four beats in each bar.

A four on the bottom means crotchet (quarter note) beats, so each bar has equal to four crotchet beats in it.

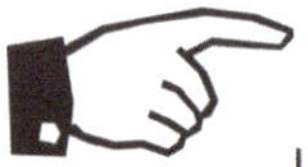

14. Clap and count:

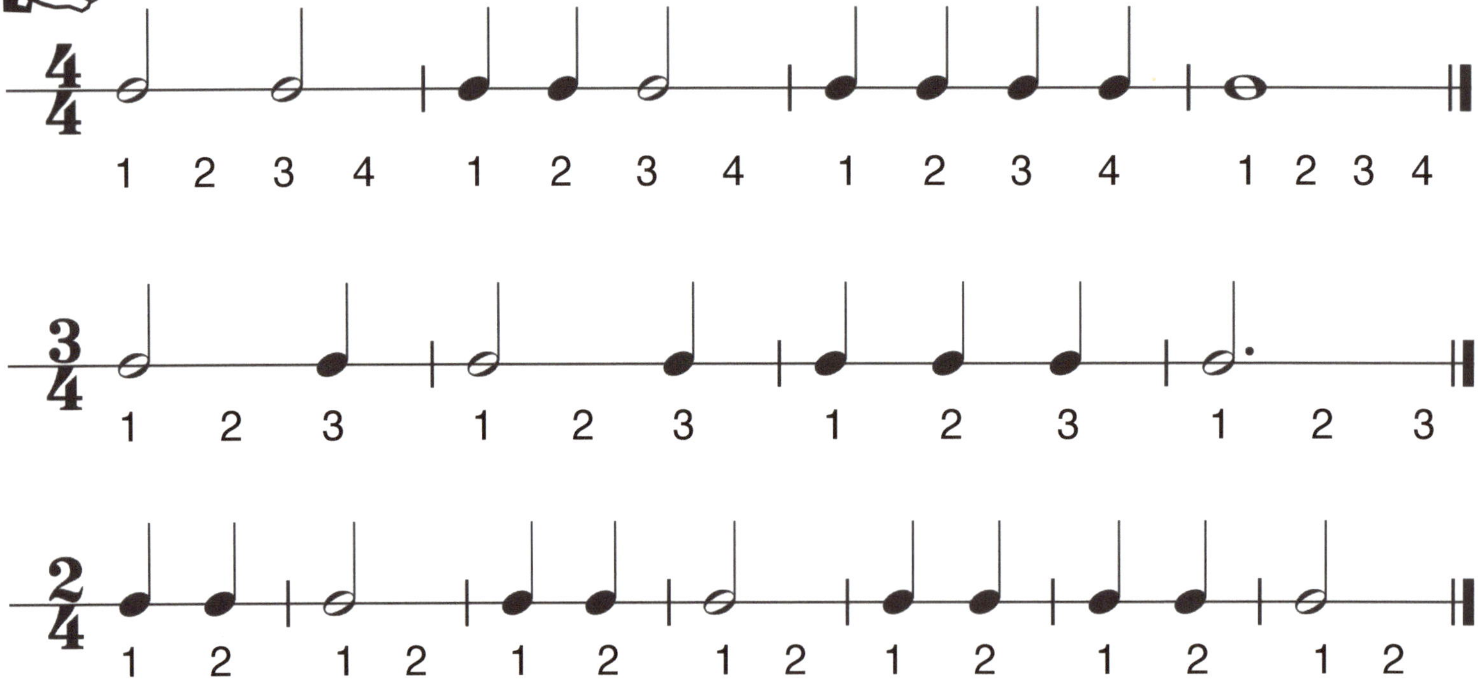

Circle the TIME SIGNATURE and decide how many beats are in each bar.

Draw the missing barlines so that every bar has the correct number of beats.

15. Each bar has ☐ beats.

16. Each bar has ☐ beats.

17. Each bar has ☐ beats.

18. Each bar has ☐ beats.

19. Each bar has ☐ beats.

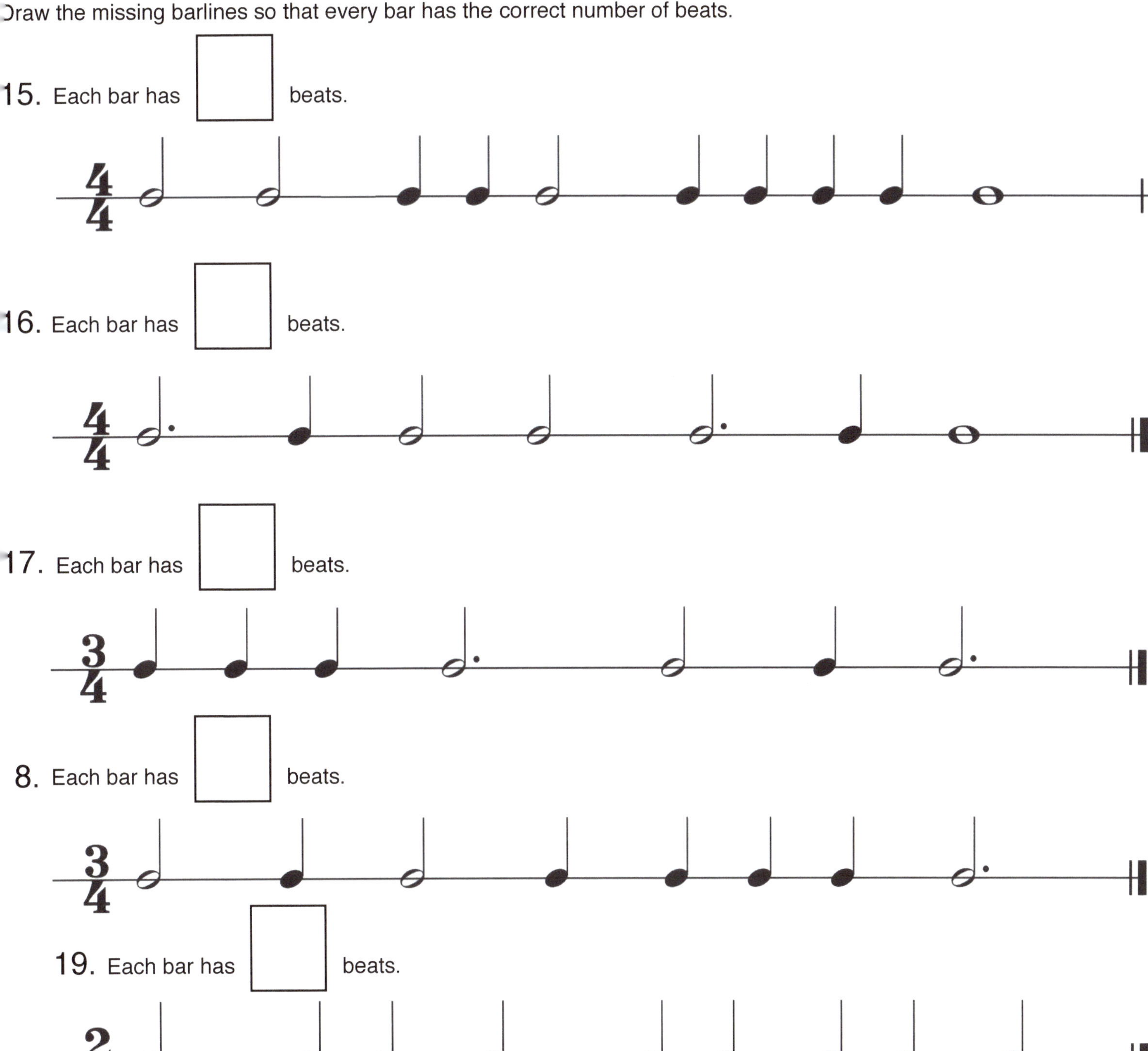

The Staff

We write music on five lines and four spaces. This is called the STAFF or STAVE.

Count the lines from
the bottom up.

Count the spaces from
the bottom up.

20. Number the lines and spaces, starting from the bottom and going up (copy the example above).

We draw notes around the lines and within the spaces.   See how the space notes sit inside each space?

21. Draw SEMIBREVES or WHOLE NOTES on the lines and in the spaces (copy the example above).

22. Write L under the LINE notes and S under the SPACE notes.

23. Draw LINE and SPACE notes on the staff above the letters.

L   S   S   L   L   S   L   S

S   L   L   S   L   S   S   L

The Staff

Remember the STAFF is like a musical ladder.

As the notes step higher up the staff, their pitch sounds higher.

Notes written at the top of the staff sound higher than notes written at the bottom of the staff.

This note sounds higher.

This note sounds lower.

Notes written on the same line or in the same space sound the same.

They have the same pitch.

These notes sound the same.

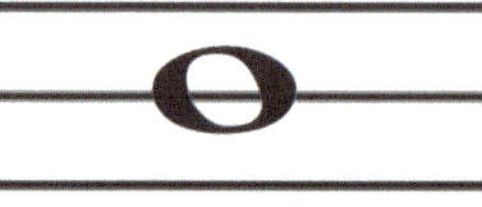

29. For each pair of notes, circle the one that sounds HIGHER.

30. For each pair of notes, circle the one that sounds LOWER.

31. For each group of notes, write down whether they are going DOWN, UP or staying the SAME.

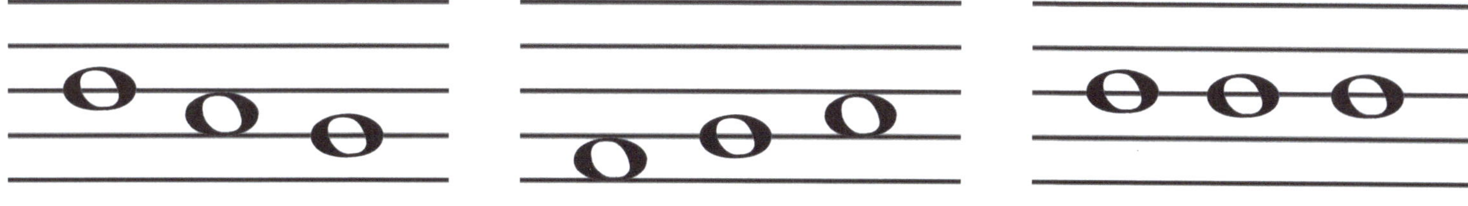

Stem direction on the staff.

On the middle line the stem
can go either up OR down

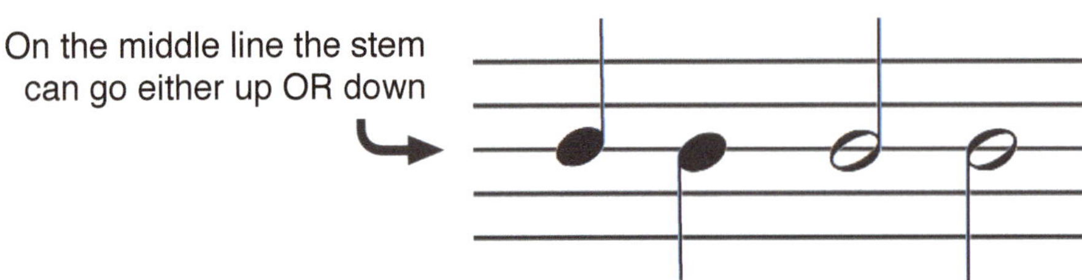

Below the middle line, stems go UP.

Above the middle line, stems go down.

32. Draw crotchets (quarter notes) and minims (half notes) BELOW the middle line (stems going up).

33. Draw crotchets (quarter notes) and minims (half notes) ABOVE the middle line

26. Circle the time signature a decide how many beats are in each bar.

Write the counts under the notes (the first example has been started for you).

Clap and count the rhythms aloud.

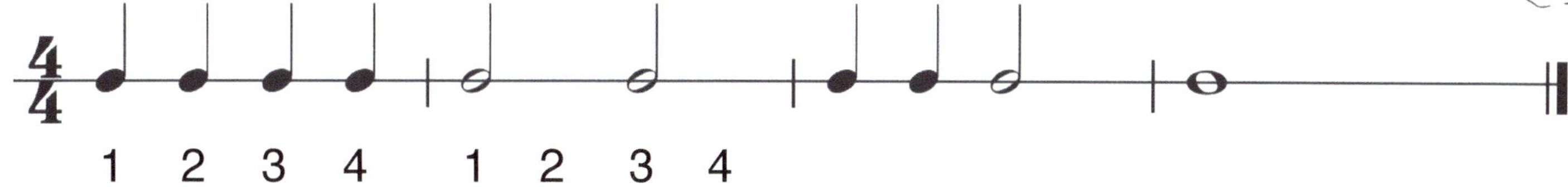

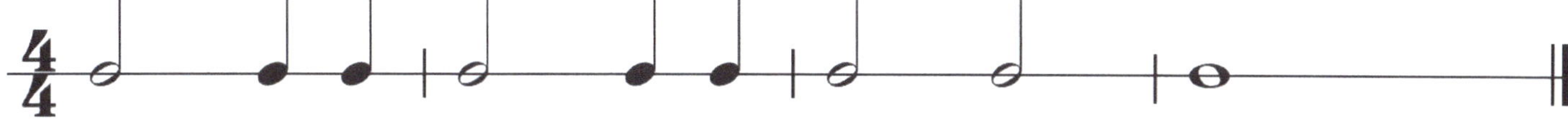

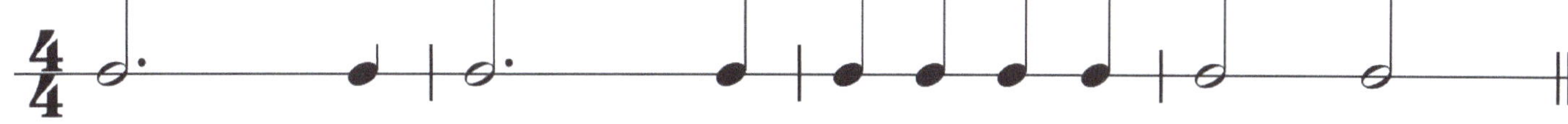

27. Write the counts under the notes (the first example has been started for you).

Clap and count the rhythms aloud.

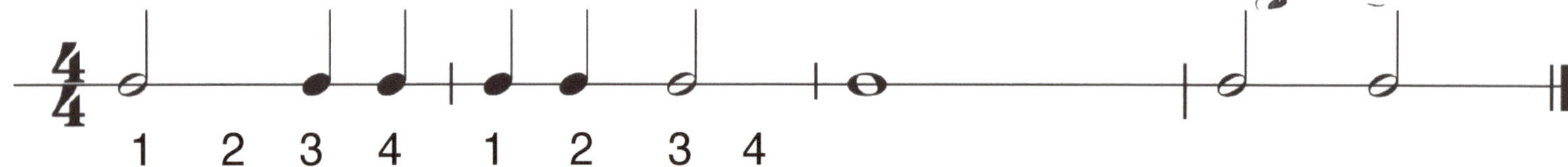

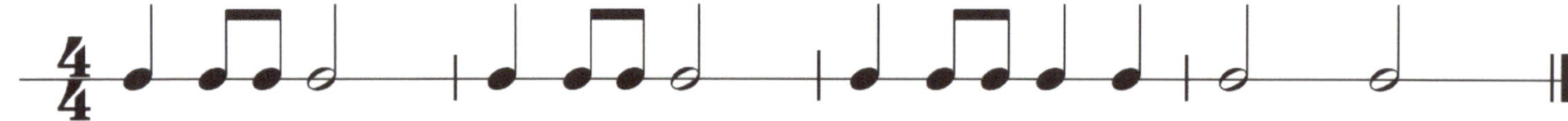

In treble clef music the note **B** is written on the middle line, like this:

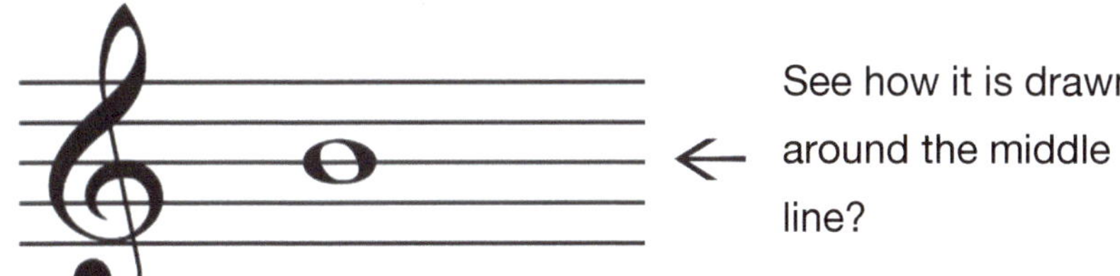

See how it is drawn
← around the middle
line?

35. Draw **B**s around the middle line:

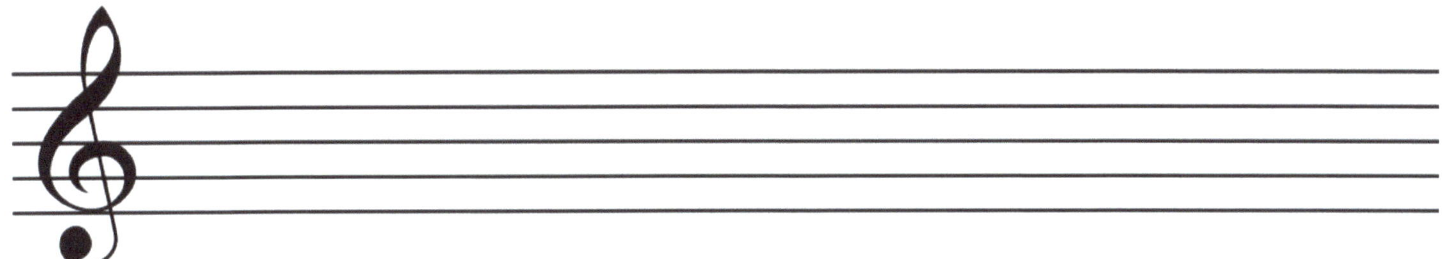

36. Circle all the **B**s in this line of music.

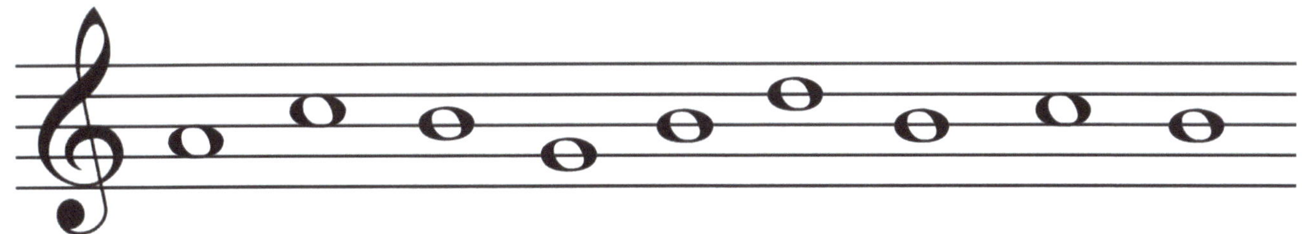

In treble clef music the note **A** is written in the second space, like this:

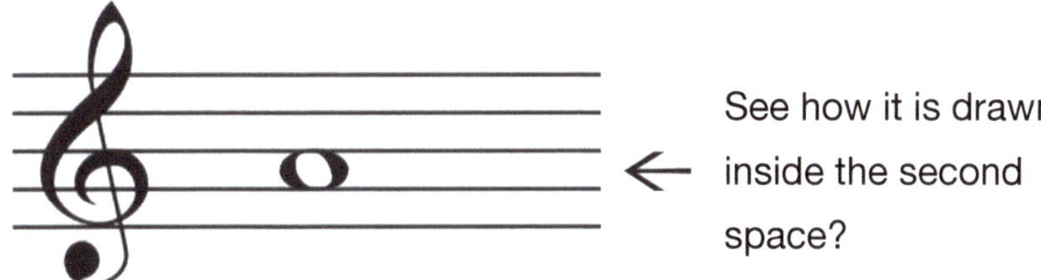

See how it is drawn
← inside the second
space?

37. Draw **A**s in the second space:

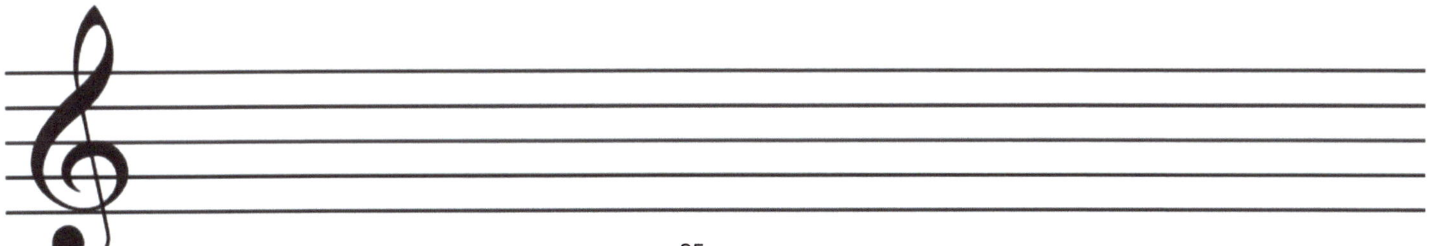

38. Circle all the **A**s in this line of music.

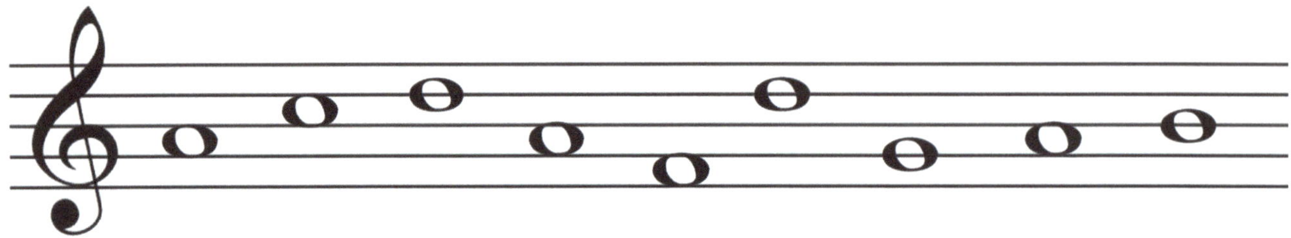

In treble clef music the note **G** is written on the second line, like this:

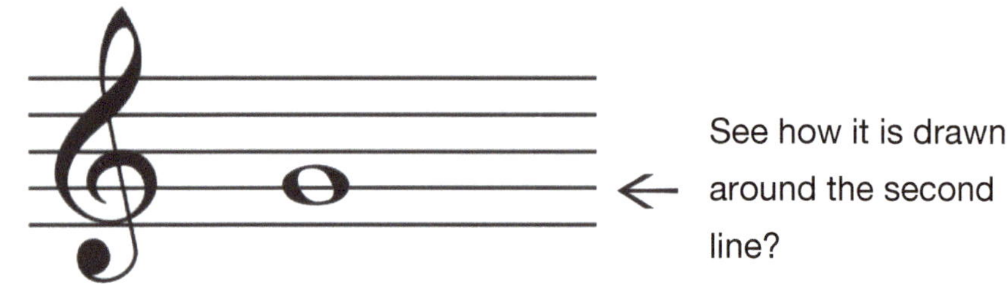

See how it is drawn ← around the second line?

39. Draw **G**s on the second line:

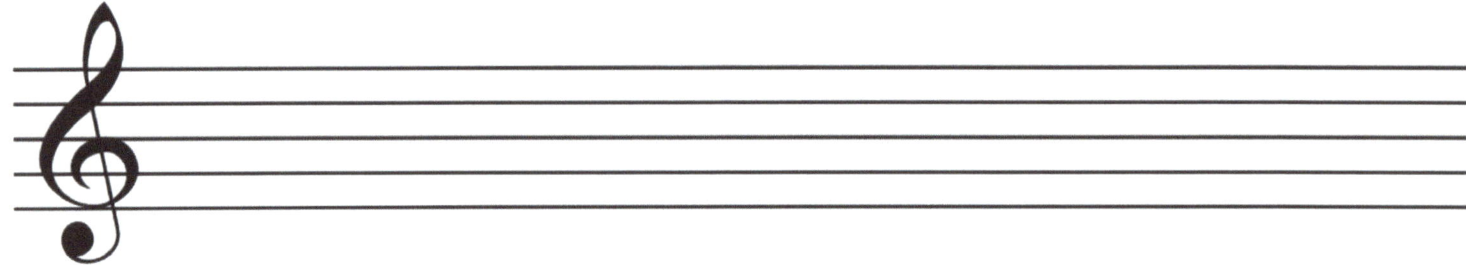

40. Circle all the **G**s in this line of music.

These exercises are intentionally left blank so that teachers can choose which notes to write.

In treble clef music the note ☐ is written like this:

Draw the note ☐

Circle all the ☐ in this line of music:

First Notes

These exercises are intentionally left blank so that teachers can choose which notes to write.

In treble clef music the note ☐ is written like this:

Draw the note ☐

Circle all the ☐ in this line of music:

These exercises are intentionally left blank so that teachers can choose which notes to write.

In treble clef music the note [ ] is written like this:

Draw the note [ ]

Circle all the [ ] in this line of music:

These exercises are intentionally left blank so that teachers can choose which notes to write.

In treble clef music the note [ ] is written like this:

Draw the note [ ]

Circle all the [ ] in this line of music:

41. Write **U** for a step UP and **D** for a step DOWN.

Write **R** if the note is repeated.

42. Draw steps in the direction indicated.

Skips

Notes that SKIP (or JUMP), skip over their next door neighbour!

A skip goes from line to line, or from space to space.

You will notice a gap on the staff between these notes.

Notes can skip up or down.

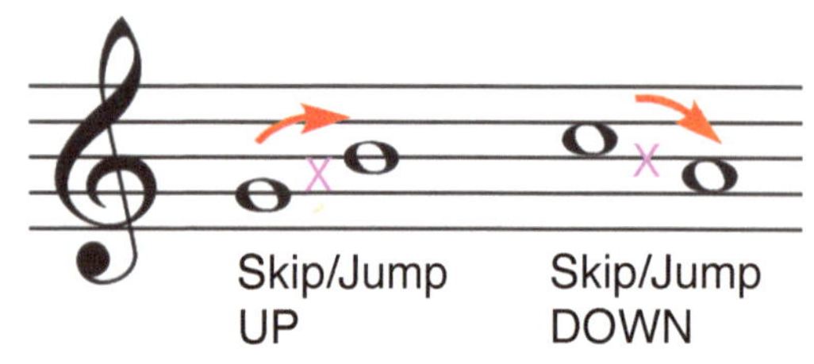

43. Write **U** for a skip UP and **D** for a skip DOWN.

44. Draw skips in the direction indicated.

15. Circle all the SKIPS.

Write:

U for a skip UP,

D for a skip DOWN,

R for a repeated note.

16. Circle all the STEPS.

Write **U** for a step UP and **D** for a step DOWN.

Write **R** for a repeated note.

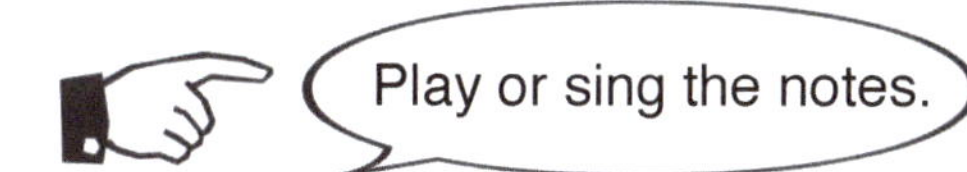

Treble Clef

This is a TREBLE CLEF.

A treble clef at the beginning of a piece of music tells us that the music is played by an instrument with a high sounding voice.

A treble clef is also known as a G CLEF, because it starts on the G LINE (the second line) and wraps around this line.

The treble clef (or G clef) starts on the G line.

34. Draw treble clefs.

Start on the G line and circle around it before curling up to the top and coming back down through the middle.

Trace around the first ones and then try drawing your own.

You can work out the letter names for the lines and spaces on the STAFF using steps and skips.

Remember, the treble clef is also known as a G CLEF, because it starts on the G LINE (the second line) and wraps around this line.

The treble clef (or G clef) starts on the G line. →

See how the letter names skip up from line to line, or fron space to space:

Skips from line to line.

Skips from space to space.

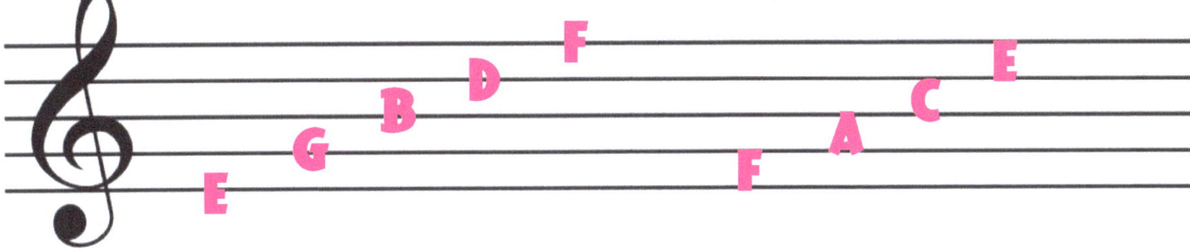

See how the letter names step up from line to space, and space to line.

51. Point to the letter names above and say (or sing) each one.

Treble Clef Notes

52. Write the letter names on the lines.

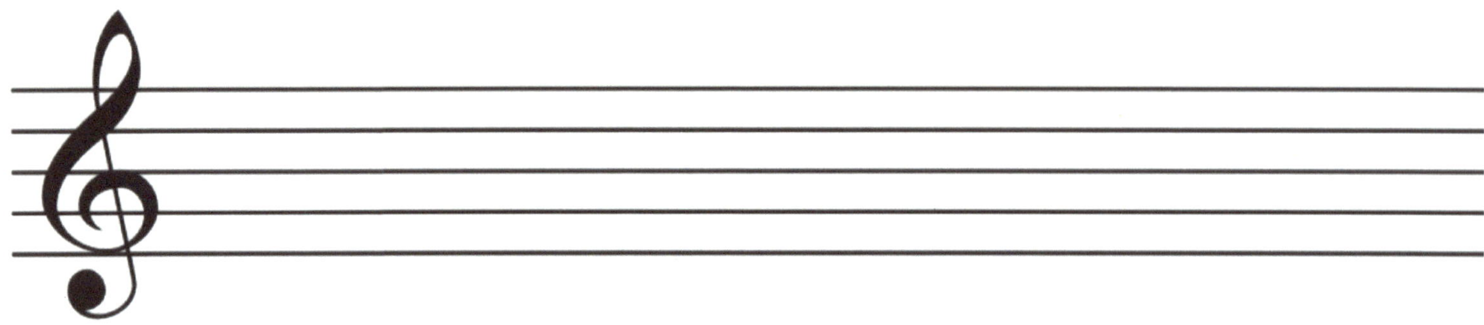

53. Write the letter names in the spaces.

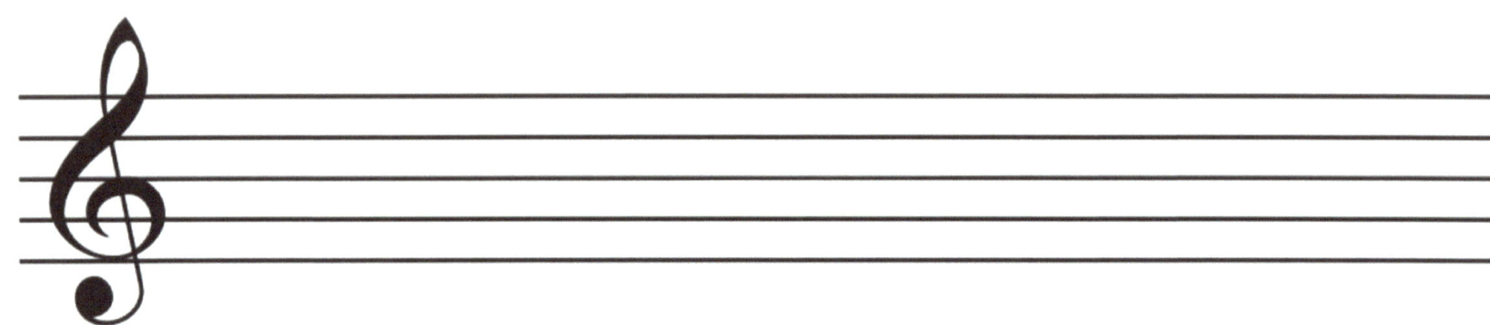

54. Write the letter names under the LINE notes.

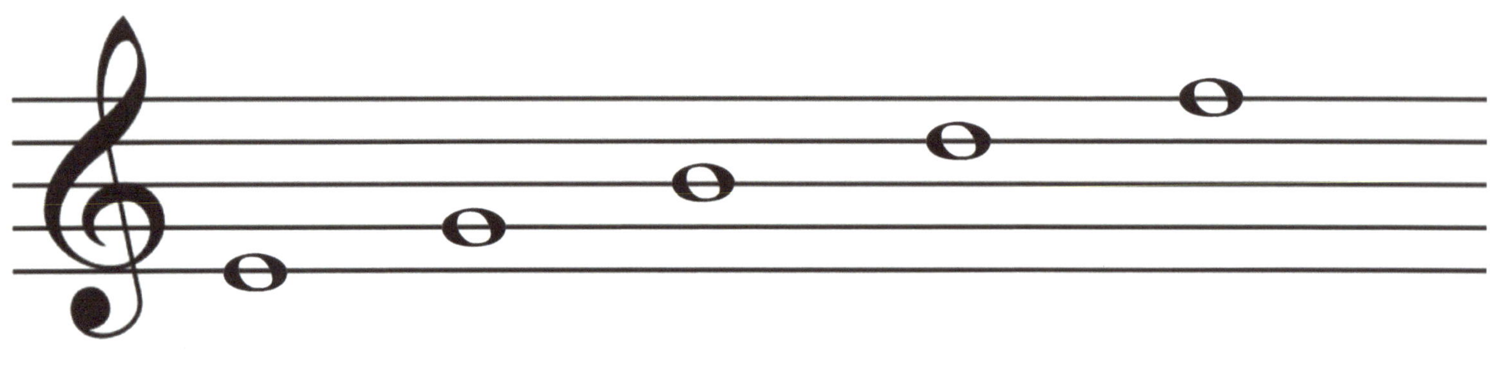

55. Write the letter names under the space notes.

____________   ____________   ____________   ____________

You can remember the letter names for the LINE notes like this:

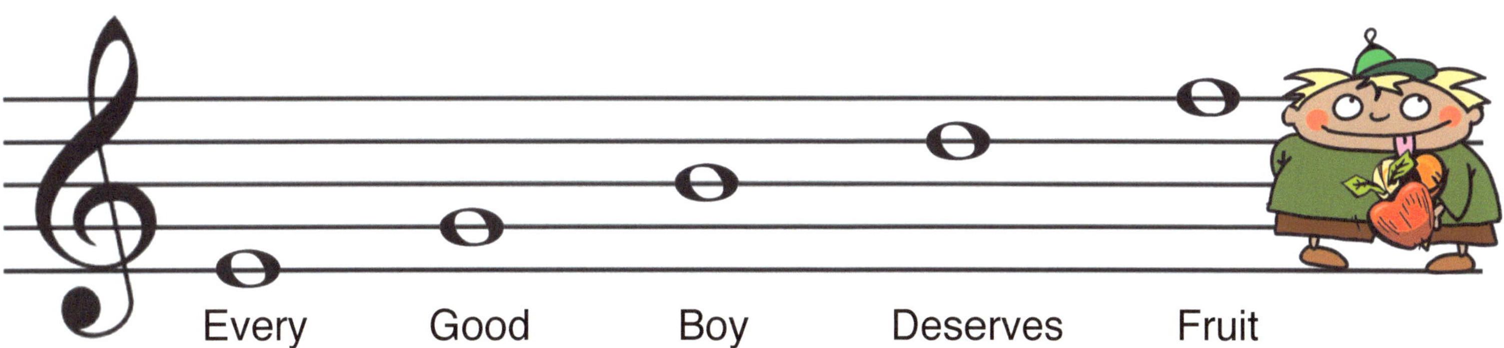

You can remember the letter names for the SPACE notes like this:

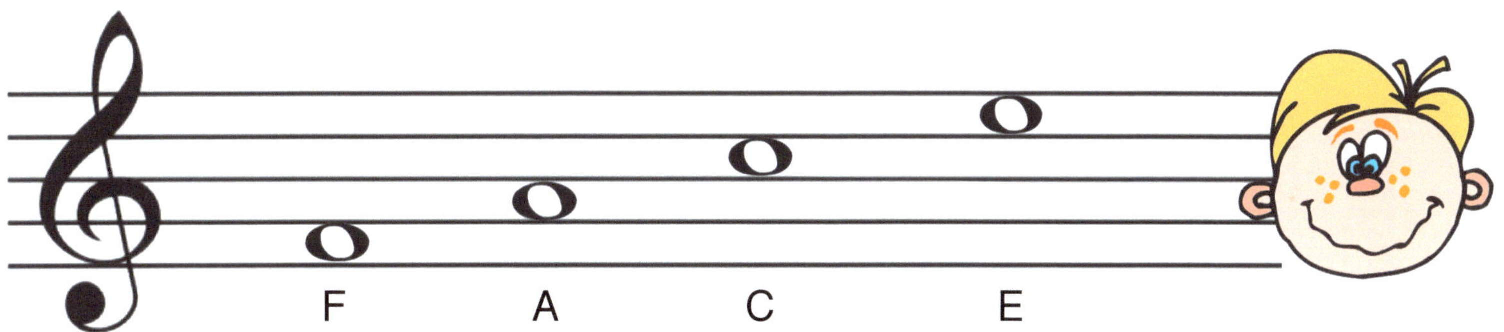

Crack the Code

56. Write the letter names under the notes to spell words.

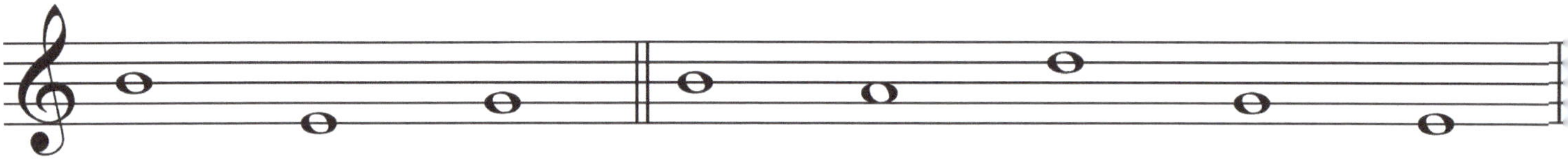

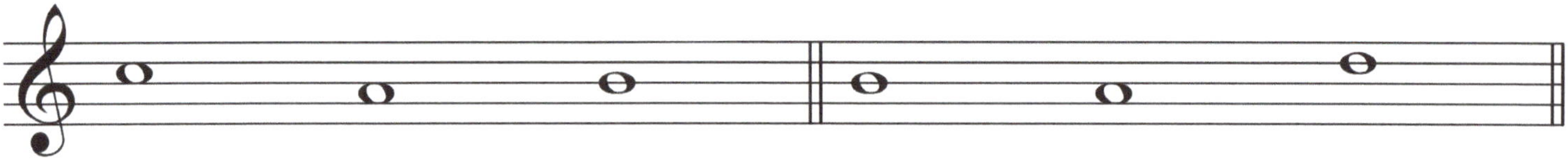

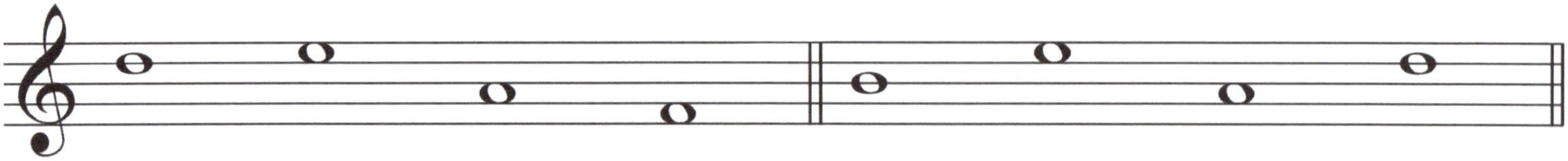

57. Write these words using notes.

58. Write the letter names under the notes to spell words.

59. Write these words using notes.

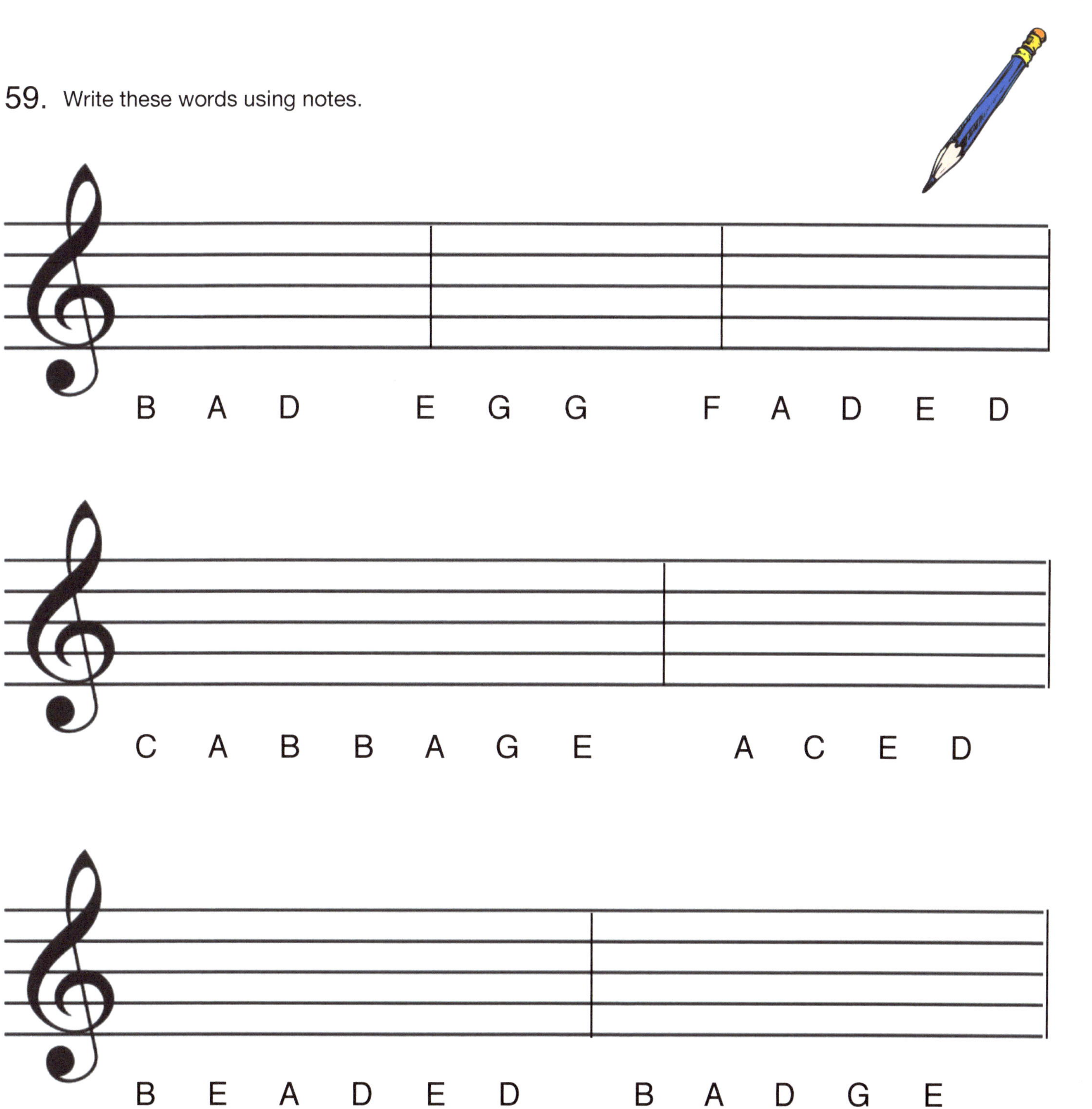

60. Write the letter names under the notes to spell words.

61. Write these words using notes.

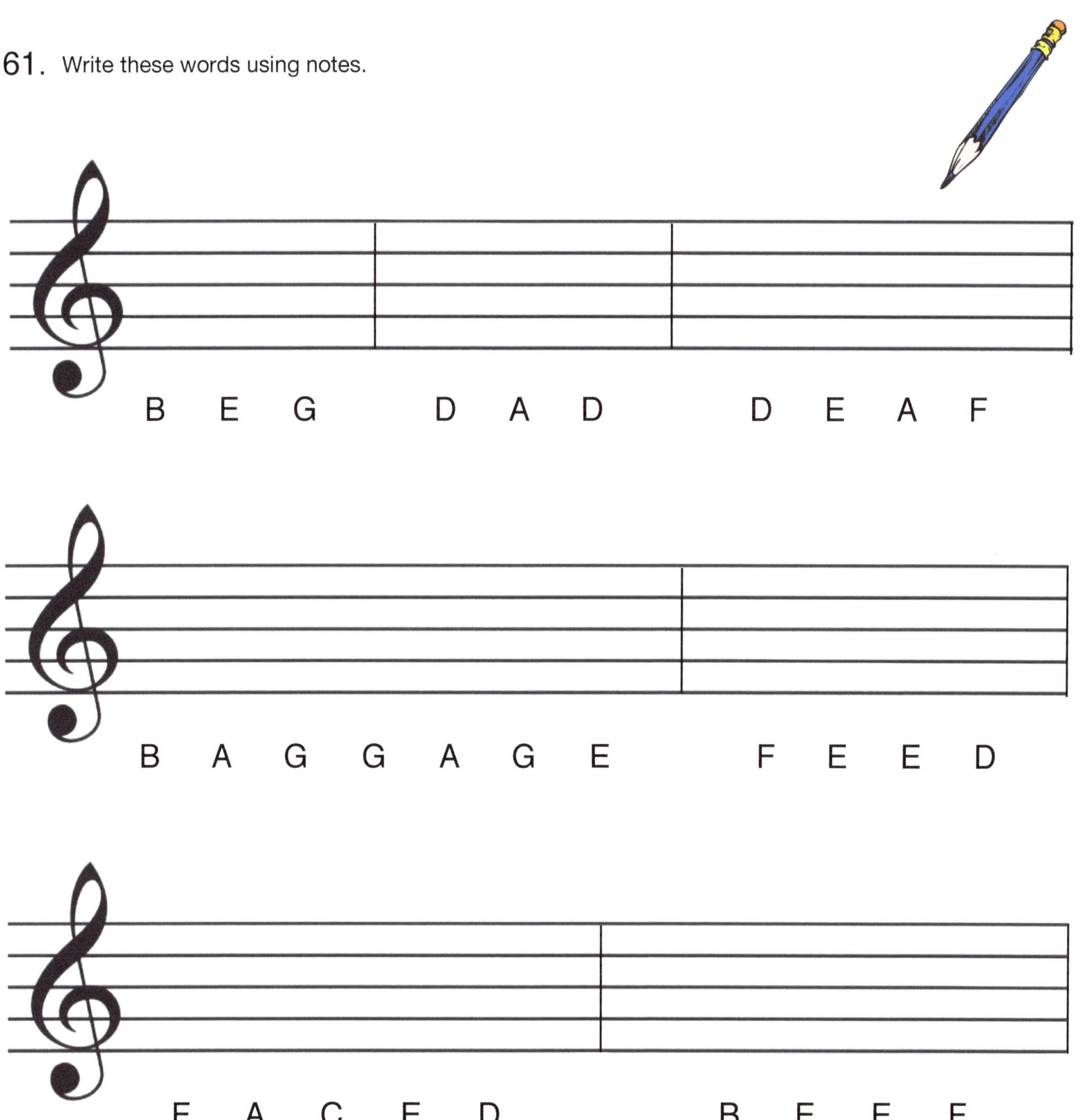

Crack the Code

62. Write the letter names under the notes to spell words.

Ledger Lines

Ledger lines are small lines used to write notes that go higher or lower than the staff.

These ledger lines are for high notes written above the staff.

These ledger lines are for low notes written below the staff.

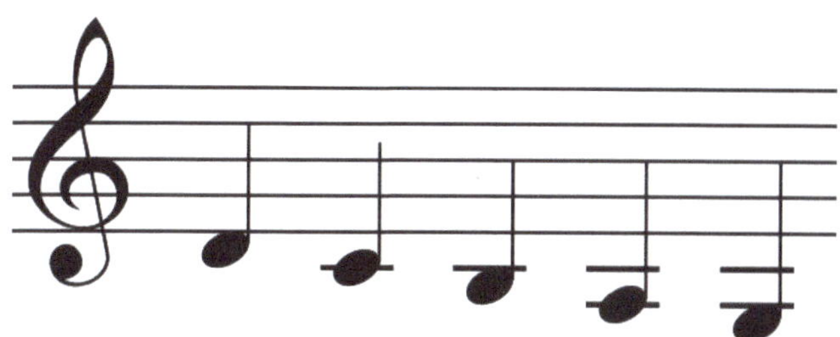

Notes on Ledger lines can be line notes or space notes.

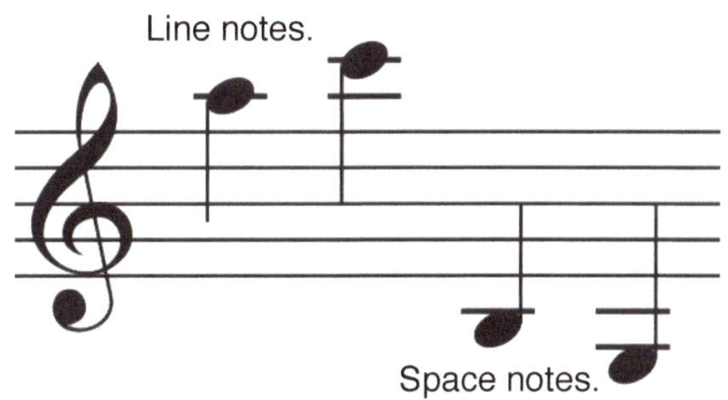

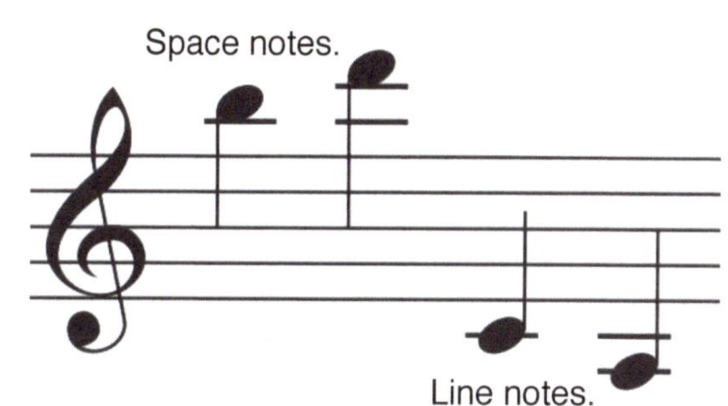

63. Write **S** under the space notes, and **L** under the line notes.

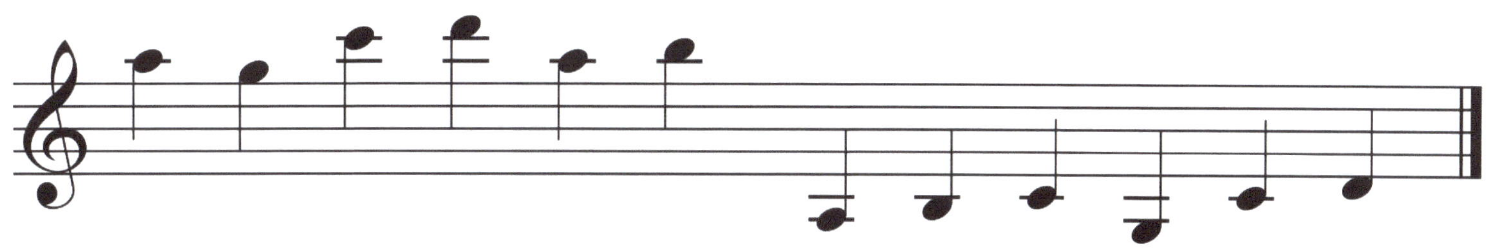

Ledger Lines

Using the musical alphabet you can work out the letter names for the notes on ledger lines.

Move by step from the top (or bottom) note of the staff.

Each step goes up, or down, one letter name.

64. Write the note a STEP UP from the given note. Write the letter names underneath.

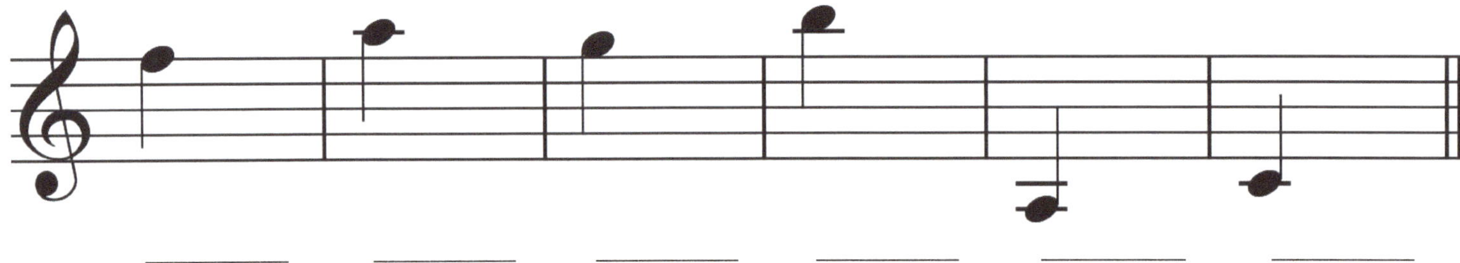

65. Write the note a STEP DOWN from the given note. Write the letter names underneath.

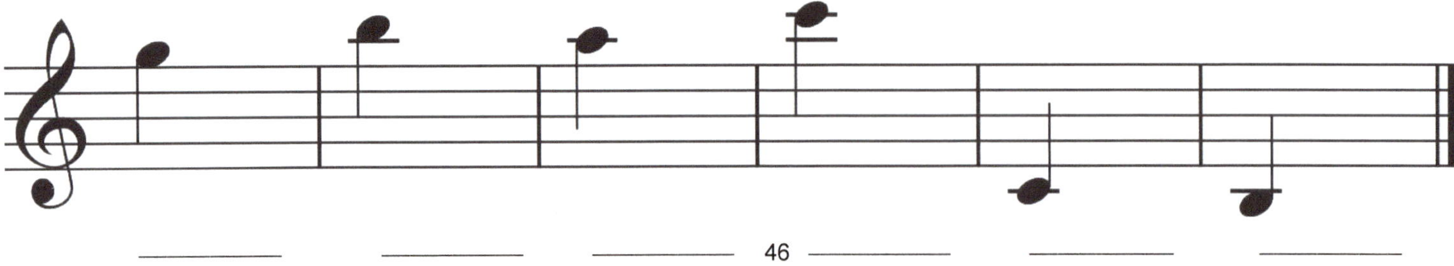

66. Write a note a SKIP UP from the given note. Write the letter names underneath.

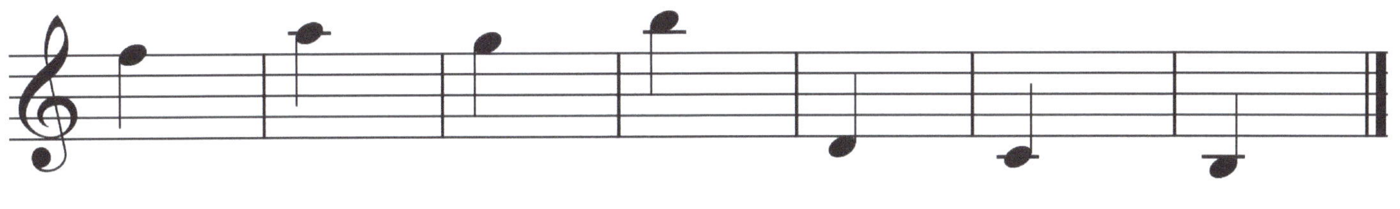

67. Write a note a SKIP DOWN from the given note. Write the letter names underneath.

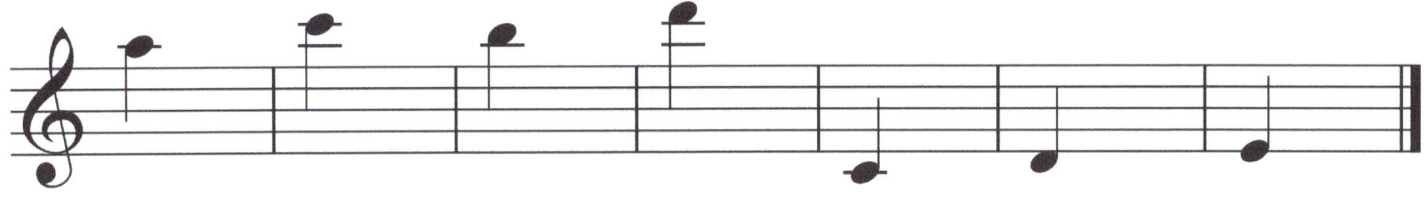

68. Write the letter names under the notes to spell words.